Men, Women and Children
in
Ancient
Egypt

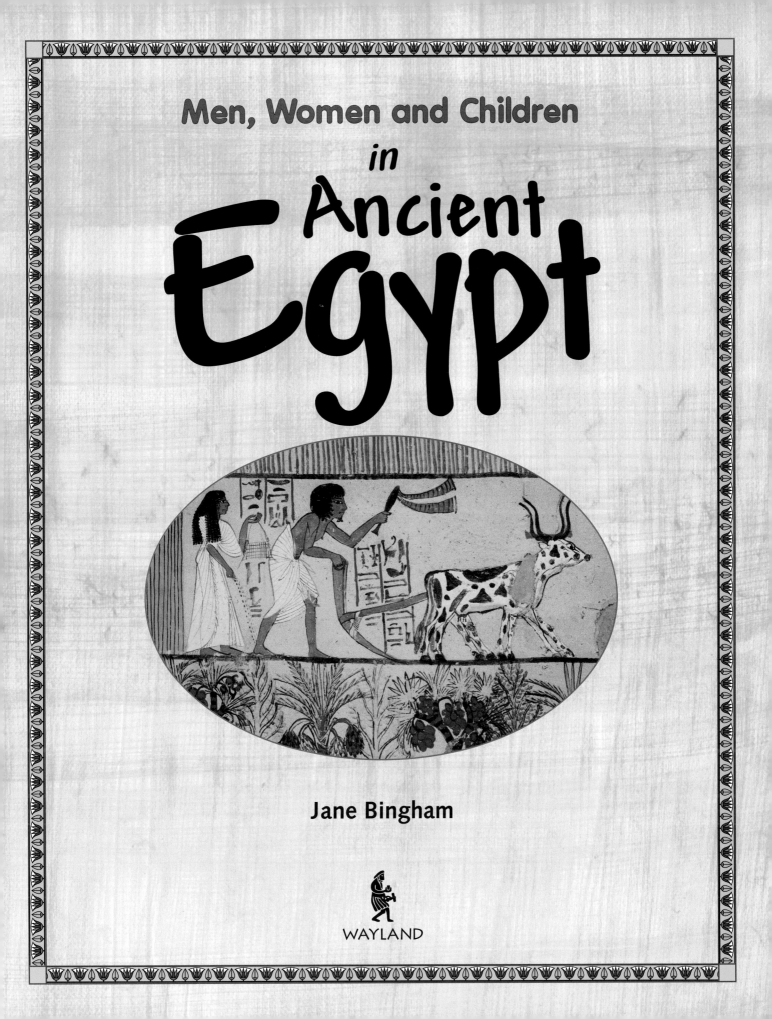

Jane Bingham

WAYLAND

First published in 2007 by Wayland, a division of Hachette Children's Books, an Hachette UK company. www.hachette.co.uk
This paperback edition published in 2009 by Wayland
Copyright © Wayland 2007

Wayland, 338 Euston Road, London NW1 3BH

Wayland Australia, Hachette Children's Books
Level 17/207 Kent Street
Sydney, NSW 2000

British Library Cataloguing in
Publication Data
Bingham, Jane
   Ancient Egypt. - (Men, women and children)
   1. Egypt - Social life and customs - To 322 B.C. - Juvenile literature
   2. Egypt - Social conditions - Juvenile literature
   I. Title
   932

ISBN: 978-0-7502-5906-4

Printed in China

Cover (main image): Queen Nefertiti was the chief wife of Pharaoh Akhaten and the mother of six daughters. Here she wears a simple crown and a wide bead necklace.

Picture acknowledgments: ARPL/HIP/Topfoto: 11; The Art Archive/Corbis: 3, 18; Bettmann/Corbis: 7; The British Library/HIP/Topfoto: 10, 14; The British Museum/Werner Forman Archive: 19; The British Museum/HIP/Topfoto: front cover tl & bl, 5, 13, 15, 24, 25; The Egyptian Museum, Cairo/Werner Forman Archive: 16; Werner Forman Archive: 26; Werner Forman Archive/Corbis: 12; Historical Picture Archive/Corbis: 22; Gianni Dagli Orti/Corbis: 17; Ronald Sheridan/AAAC: 20; Spectrum Colour Library/HIP/Topfoto:front cover cl, 9; Topfoto: 27; Charles Walker/Topfoto: front cover main, 23; Ron Watts/Corbis: 21; Roger Wood/Corbis: 8.

Map by Peter Bull.

CONTENTS

Words that appear in **bold**
can be found in the glossary
on page 28.

WHO WERE THE ANCIENT EGYPTIANS?

A map of Ancient Egypt, showing the main cities. (Modern names are shown in brackets.)

Mediterranean Sea

Alexandria

LOWER EGYPT

Giza • (Cairo)
Memphis •

SINAI

U
P
P
E
R

E
G
Y
P
T

River Nile

Red Sea

Valley of
the Kings • Thebes

• (Aswan)

(Lake Nasser)

▲ A map of Ancient Egypt, showing the main cities. (Modern names are shown in brackets.)

The Ancient Egyptians began as a race of people living on the banks of the River Nile, in North Africa. Gradually, they learnt how to grow crops and **irrigate** the land, and, by 5000 BC, they were farming the **fertile** soil beside the river. The farmers settled in villages which, over time, grew into larger communities.

EGYPT UNITES

By the 4th century BC, there were two kingdoms on the River Nile: Upper Egypt and Lower Egypt. Then, around 3100 BC, the kingdoms were united by **Pharaoh** Menes. He built a capital city at Memphis, and started a **dynasty** (or family) of powerful rulers.

THREE PERIODS

The Ancient Egyptian **civilization** lasted for over 2000 years. Historians have identified three great periods in this long history. The Old Kingdom (c.2575 –2150 BC) was the time when most of the great pyramids were built. The Middle Kingdom (c.1975-1640 BC) was the period when art and literature flourished. The New Kingdom (c.1539-1075 BC) was a time of expansion, when the Egyptians gained an empire that was at its largest in about 1450 BC.

EYGPTIAN TIMELINE

5000 BC   4000   3000

c.5000 BC Farming begins in the Nile valley.

c.3100 BC Pharaoh Menes unites Upper and Lower Egypt.

c.2575 BC Old Kingdom begins.

THE END OF THE EMPIRE

By the 1st century BC, the Egyptian Empire had started to weaken and the Egyptians had to defend themselves against many enemies. Finally, in 332 BC, they were conquered by a Greek army led by Alexander the Great. For the next 300 years, Egypt was ruled by members of the Ptolemy family, who were descended from one of Alexander's **generals**.

In 32 BC, Rome went to war with Egypt. The Egyptians were defeated and their ruler, Queen Cleopatra, killed herself. Egypt became part of the Roman Empire in 30 BC, and the great Egyptian civilization came to an end.

REAL LIVES

CLEOPATRA: THE LAST QUEEN OF EGYPT

Cleopatra (shown here) was joint ruler of Egypt, first with her father and later with her husband. After her husband died, she ruled on her own. She fell in love with a Roman general, Mark Anthony. They combined their armies to fight against the Romans, but they were defeated and Cleopatra committed suicide. Historians believe that she killed herself by applying a poisonous snake to her arm.

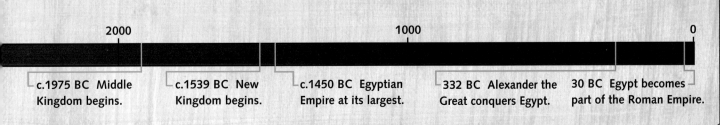

2000	1000	0

c.1975 BC Middle Kingdom begins.

c.1539 BC New Kingdom begins.

c.1450 BC Egyptian Empire at its largest.

332 BC Alexander the Great conquers Egypt.

30 BC Egypt becomes part of the Roman Empire.

EGYPTIAN MEN, WOMEN AND CHILDREN

Ancient Egyptian society was divided into two main classes: the wealthy rulers and nobles, and the ordinary working people. Men of all classes had more freedom than women, but Egyptian women had more rights than women in Ancient Greece or Rome.

EGYPTIAN MEN

Egyptian men saw themselves as the head of the household, but most of them left the job of running the home to their wives. By law, men could have as many wives as they wished, and some pharaohs had hundreds. However, most Egyptians could only afford to support one wife.

EGYPTIAN WOMEN

Women in Ancient Egypt had the right to own property and to run a business. If an Egyptian woman was accused of a crime, she could appear in court to defend herself.

Wealthy women had a large staff of servants to help them run their homes, but women from poor families did all the housework themselves, with the help of their daughters. Only a few noblewomen went out to work but poorer women often helped their husbands in the fields, or did other jobs in the community (see pages 18-21). Egyptian women of all classes were kept very busy bringing up their

▲ The most important person in Ancient Egypt was the pharaoh, or king. Ancient Egyptian pharaohs were treated like gods by their people. This painting shows Pharaoh Ramses III embracing the goddess Isis.

families. It was not unusual for a woman to give birth to ten children, although it was rare for all the children to survive.

EGYPTIAN CHILDREN

Children were greatly valued in Egyptian society and most children enjoyed a close family life. However, by the time they were 12 years old, Egyptian children were seen as adults. Girls could be married at this age, and the children from poorer families were expected to start full time work. Some Egyptian children started to work with their parents before they were even five years old.

◀ An Egyptian carving of a husband and wife. The couple seem to be fond of each other, as the wife has her arm around her husband's shoulders. The two small figures are probably their children.

REAL LIVES

NAUNAKTE: A NOBLEWOMAN

An Egyptian noblewoman, known simply as Lady Naunakte, wrote a will before she died. Naunakte clearly had property and wealth of her own, independently of her husband. In her will, she proudly announced that she had managed to provide for all her children. Naunakte wrote "I am a free woman of Egypt. I have raised eight children, and have provided them with everything suitable for their station in life."

WHO WAS IN CHARGE IN ANCIENT EGYPTIAN TIMES?

At the head of Egyptian society was the all-powerful pharaoh. He made all the important decisions about how his kingdom was run. **Ministers** helped to rule Egypt, and hundreds of **officials** ran the different regions of the Empire.

POWERFUL PHARAOHS

There were a few examples of powerful female pharaohs, but pharaohs in Ancient Egypt were almost always male. The pharaoh lived in a vast palace with his many wives and children. All the members of the royal family were treated with great respect, but the most important person, after the pharaoh, was his chief wife. The pharaoh usually chose one of his sisters to be his chief wife and her son became the next pharaoh. This way, the divine blood of the pharaohs remained as 'pure' as possible.

As well as ruling their kingdom, pharaohs also led the Egyptian army. One of the greatest warrior pharaohs was Tuthmosis III, who conquered more than 300 cities and led his army to war 17 times over a period of 25 years. Pharaohs gave orders for magnificent monuments to be built. Teams of builders constructed huge pyramids and temples in honour of the pharaohs.

▶ Pharaohs often led their armies in war. In this painting, Pharaoh Ramses II charges into battle, while his enemies fall beneath his chariot.

VIZIERS AND VICEROYS

Three important ministers helped the pharaoh to run Egypt. Two **viziers** were in charge of Upper and Lower Egypt, while a **viceroy** governed Nubia (a large territory to the south of Egypt). These three men had a large staff of officials who collected taxes, ran the law courts, and supervised farming and building projects.

GENERALS AND PRIESTS

Army generals had a lot of power in Ancient Egypt. A few very talented generals even became pharaohs themselves. High priests were also very powerful figures. It was believed that they could interpret the will of the gods, and so they were often asked to advise the pharaoh.

REAL LIVES

TUTANKHAMUN: A BOY PHARAOH

Tutankhamun was the son of Pharaoh Akhenaten. When he was about nine years old, his father died, so Tutankhamun became pharaoh. Around this time he was married to his half-sister Ankhesenamun, who was slightly older than him. Because Tutankhamun was so young, two adult **regents** ruled for him. He died when he was about 19, probably from a broken leg that became infected. Tutankhamun's mummified body was preserved inside a magnificent set of coffin cases, one of which is shown here.

WHAT WAS LIFE LIKE IN AN EGYPTIAN FAMILY?

Most Egyptian families were much larger than families today. An Egyptian household usually consisted of an older married couple and their sons, who each had their own wife and children. Wealthy families also had servants to help them run their home. As well as all these people, there were often animals running around the house: cats, dogs and monkeys were popular family pets.

FAMILY HOMES

Rich Egyptians lived in large villas with many rooms and a central hall for entertaining guests. The rooms were furnished with wooden tables, chairs and beds. Villas often had shady gardens and pools and were sometimes surrounded by their own farming lands.

Ordinary families had simple cottages with just a few rooms. The same room was used for eating and sleeping, and benches around the sides of the room could be used as seats or beds.

▲ Wealthy Egyptian families often lived in villas, surrounded by farmland. This painting shows servants at work in a villa and on its farm.

HUSBANDS AND WIVES

Egyptian girls were usually married in their early teens. Boys often waited to marry until they were around 20 years old and they had become established in their work. Divorce was easy in Egyptian society – both partners had the right to ask the courts to end a marriage. However there is evidence that most couples stayed together for life.

FAMILY SERVANTS

Rich people kept a large staff of servants to help them run their villas and the surrounding lands. Within the home, servants cooked and cleaned and repaired the family's clothes. They also waited on their master and mistress, and helped to care for the children.

▲ A young Egyptian couple from the ruling class. The couple share a carved throne, and they are finely dressed in pleated robes and heavy wigs.

REAL LIVES

MEKET-RE: A VILLA OWNER

Meket-Re was an important Egyptian official who lived in the 3rd century BC. His tomb contains painted wooden models of his family home with its gardens and pool, and also its kitchens, workshops and grain stores. One set of models shows Meket-Re with his son and four scribes, counting the cattle on his estate. The models provide a fascinating picture of the home life of a leading member of the Egyptian ruling class.

BABIES AND YOUNG CHILDREN

In Ancient Egypt, one in five children died before they reached their teens, so people did everything they could to keep them safe. Parents tried to protect their children with prayers and spells, and babies and children wore amulets (lucky charms) around their neck.

Mothers from ordinary families cared for their own children, often breastfeeding them until they were three years old. Wealthy women paid poorer mothers to do the job of breastfeeding their babies.

BOYS AND GIRLS

From an early age, boys and girls were kept apart. Wealthy boys learnt how to read and write. Boys from ordinary families trained to do the same work as their father. A son might work beside his father in the fields, or learn the family trade in a workshop.

Girls of all classes stayed at home with their mothers. Wealthy girls learnt how to run a household and supervise slaves. Girls from poor families were expected to help look after their younger sisters and brothers. They also learnt how to cook and clean, and how to spin and weave cloth to make the family's clothes.

◄ A pharaoh and his teacher. This painting shows a young ruler sitting on the lap of his female tutor. Wealthy Egyptians were often taught at home.

CHILDREN'S TOYS

Young children played with wooden balls, dolls and spinning tops. They also had model animals made from clay or wood. Some of these animals had moving parts that were worked by pulling a string.

▲ Egyptian children played with simple wooden dolls like this. The doll is painted with colourful designs and has mud beads for hair.

REAL LIVES

"SHERIT": A MUCH-LOVED CHILD

Archaeologists have recently examined the **mummy** of a young Egyptian girl. They discovered that she had long curly hair and was between four and six years old. They also found she had been breast fed until about a year before she died. No expense had been spared on the little girl's funeral. She wore a golden face mask, and her body had been carefully prepared for burial – almost certainly by her loving parents. The girl's body shows no sign of injury, so she may have died from an infectious disease or from food poisoning (both very common causes of death). Her real name is not known, but archaeologists have called her Sherit, an Egyptian name that means "little one".

Did Egyptian children go to school?

Most Egyptian children did not go to school. Children in poor families had to help their parents with their work, and rich boys and girls often had a private tutor to teach them at home. However, there were some schools attached to the temples, although they only took boys.

Temple schools

Some temple schools were attached to important temples in the cities, and only took boys from the ruling classes. There were also smaller temple schools in the villages. The village schools were open to all boys, but they were expensive so families had to save up to send their sons to school.

Boys started at temple school when they were around five years old. For the first few years, they concentrated on copying texts and reading aloud. The teachers at the temple schools were very strict and pupils were often beaten for not working hard enough.

Older pupils studied more advanced texts, such as the *Book of Wisdom*, which gave advice to young men on how to behave. Later, some students specialized in different subjects such as mathematics, religion, engineering or medicine.

▲ The Ancient Egyptians did not have an alphabet. Instead, they used a system of picture signs – known as **hieroglyphs** - to write things down. The hieroglyphs shown here were painted on a coffin.

EGYPTIAN WRITING

Egyptian writing was very hard to learn because it was made up of more than 700 picture signs called hieroglyphs. Some of the hieroglyphs represent an object or a person. Others represent a sound.

School pupils wrote with a reed pen dipped in ink. They practised their writing on pieces of broken pottery or flakes of stone that could be thrown away. By the end of their schooling, they were ready to write on **papyrus** – a kind of fine white paper made from reeds.

SCRIBES

Many pupils at temple schools later became **scribes**. This was a very important job, and scribes had a high position in Egyptian society. They kept all the records needed to run the kingdom of Egypt. They also wrote the histories of the pharaohs and their deeds.

▼ A carving of the scribe Amenhotep at work. Amenhotep sits cross-legged to write on his scroll, using his stretched-out kilt as a desk.

REAL LIVES

AMENHOTEP: A ROYAL SCRIBE

Amenhotep was a very well educated man. He was the special scribe of Pharaoh Amenhotep III, but also an architect, priest, teacher and healer. He drew out the plans for the pharaoh's massive building projects and organized their construction. After his death, he became famous for his teachings. Amenhotep was eventually worshipped as a god of healing.

What Jobs did Egyptian People Do?

Most Egyptians were farmers on the banks of the River Nile. Many others worked as fishermen, weavers or potters. Educated people had jobs as government officials, priests, scribes and doctors. Merchants made long journeys to exchange goods, and men of all classes joined the army.

Women's Work

Most Egyptian women stayed at home, but a few had careers. Noblewomen could become priestesses. They could also work as singers, dancers and musicians in the temples. Poorer women had jobs as weavers in workshops, or as servants to the rich. Women from farming families worked with the men in the fields.

▼ Egyptian couples often worked together in the fields. Here, the husband ploughs the earth and scares away the birds, while his wife follows, sowing seeds.

Slave Labour

By the time of the New Kingdom, slavery was common. Many slaves were prisoners-of-war from the lands that the Egyptians had won for their Empire (see pages 6-7). They were often employed as builders, miners, or household servants. Some slaves had very hard lives, but others were well treated. A few slaves were set free and some of them married local people.

Working on the Land

Egyptian farmers grew a range of vegetables, figs, dates and grapes but their main crop was wheat. Most of the land was used for crops, but farmers also kept some animals, such as sheep, pigs, goats, geese and ducks. Oxen were used as working animals, and only rich farmers reared cows to eat.

CRAFT WORKERS

Skilled Egyptian craft workers produced a wide range of goods. Potters worked with clay, or carved pots from stone, and carpenters used local and imported woods to make furniture and statues. Metalworkers made tools and weapons, and jewellers created elaborate pieces from silver and gold, beads and precious stones. Craft workers sometimes worked in a family group, or as part of a team in a large workshop.

▲ This painting shows a jewellery workshop. The workers are boring holes in beads, polishing the beads, and threading them onto a wide collar.

REAL LIVES

ASRU: A SINGER

A coffin has survived from Ancient Egypt containing the mummified body of a working woman. The coffin **inscription** says that she was Asru, a singer in a temple. Archaeologists believe Asru was at least 60 when she died. This was unusual in Egyptian times, when most women did not survive beyond 40. Asru's long life was probably due to the fact that she had a safe and comfortable life working in a temple.

BUILDING TEMPLES AND PYRAMIDS

Thousands of Egyptians worked on the massive pyramids and temples of Ancient Egypt. Miners cut stone from quarries, while stonecutters shaped it into blocks. Then teams of workers hauled the blocks onto sledges and took them to where they were needed. Builders set the massive stones in place and masons trimmed them to fit.

ARMY LIFE

By the time of the New Kingdom, Egypt had a large professional army. The ordinary soldiers came from the lower classes, but officers were always educated, wealthy men. Life in the Egyptian army was tough. Soldiers were sent on long marches and had to train very hard. Egyptian soldiers carried spears and shields, but they had no protective armour so they suffered terrible injuries.

DOCTORS

Egyptian doctors were famous throughout the Middle East for their skill. They studied medical texts and specialized in different areas of the body, such as the stomach, the teeth or the head. Doctors performed surgery, sewed up cuts, set broken limbs and treated wounds. They also made medicines from plants and **minerals** and even animal parts. If these methods failed to work, doctors also tried to use spells and magic charms to help them cure their patients.

▼ This painting shows workmen pulling blocks of stone on a sledge. The man at the back of the group is probably the foreman, who gave orders to the workers.

An embalmer prepares a body for burial. The embalmer wears a mask carved with the head of Anubis, the god of the dead.

EMBALMERS

The Egyptians believed in life after death. They thought that the dead would need their bodies in the **next world**, so they preserved the bodies as **mummies**. The people who did this important work were known as **embalmers**. They worked in tents beside the River Nile.

Embalmers prepared the bodies of the dead for burial. First, they removed the brains and **internal organs** and stored them in jars. Then they covered the body with a salt called natron to help it dry out. When the body was thoroughly dry, its insides were stuffed with a mixture of linen, sawdust, and sweet-smelling spices. Finally, the embalmers wrapped the mummy in layers of bandages, and placed it in a coffin, ready to be buried in a tomb.

REAL LIVES

IMHOTEP: A MAN WITH MANY JOBS

Imhotep was the architect of Egypt's first pyramid, which was built for Pharaoh Djoser. He was also the **chancellor** of Egypt, and ran the kingdom's finances. However these were not his only jobs. Imhotep also worked as a **high priest**, a sculptor, and a doctor!

WHAT DID EGYPTIAN ADULTS AND CHILDREN WEAR?

In the hot, dry climate of Ancient Egypt people did not need many clothes. In fact, most children went naked until they were in their teens. Most Egyptians wore simple clothes, but added a lot of jewellery to make themselves look good.

▲ Most Egyptians dressed very simply, in kilts for the men and long tunic-dresses for the women. Women's tunics were usually white, but sometimes they were dyed dramatic colours.

CHANGING STYLES

Until the time of the New Kingdom, all the Egyptians wore the same basic clothes. Men wore a simple kilt, made from a piece of linen wrapped around the waist. Women wore a long tunic that reached to their ankles. Wealthy people's clothes were made from fine linen, while ordinary people used a thicker, coarser cloth. People of all classes wore sandals made from reeds.

In the New Kingdom, styles changed. Fashionable people wore cloaks made from very thin, pleated linen. Some men wore a double kilt (one long and one short) and women's tunics were decorated with ornaments and fringes.

LOOKING GOOD

Rich men and women spent a lot of time on their looks. They bathed every day and rubbed scented oils on their skin. Both sexes wore heavy eye make-up. They believed that it protected their eyes from the glare of the sun and prevented eye disease. For special occasions, men and women wore heavy wigs, decorated with beads and jewels.

All Egyptians liked to wear jewellery, and both men and women wore necklaces, bracelets and earrings. Wealthy people wore jewellery made from gold and precious stones. Poor people's jewellery was made from copper and beads.

▶ A carving of the elegant Queen Nefertiti. Here, the queen wears a simple crown and a wide bead necklace.

A SPECIAL HAIRSTYLE

Egyptian children had their own special hairstyle. Their hair was shaved off or kept very short except for a lock on the side of the head. This long, s-shaped curl was called the "side-lock of youth". Children wore this style until they were around 12 years old, when they were considered to be adults.

REAL LIVES

NEFERTITI: A BEAUTIFUL QUEEN

Nefertiti was the chief wife of Pharaoh Akhaten and the mother of six daughters. In carvings, she is shown as very beautiful, with a long, slim neck and carefully made-up eyes and lips. Some carvers show her standing beside the pharaoh as his equal, and this probably means she had great influence over her husband.

How did Egyptian adults and children have fun?

People in Ancient Egypt really liked to enjoy themselves. Wealthy Egyptians held lavish banquets, with music and dancing. Kings and nobles hunted for sport, and people of all classes played sports and games.

Egyptian parties

Rich Egyptians held large parties. They provided banquets with many courses and laid on plenty of entertainments. During the feast, musicians played on harps, flutes, pipes and drums. Later in the evening, singers, dancers, jugglers and acrobats entertained the guests.

Hunting and fishing

Hunting and fishing were popular sports for wealthy Egyptians. Nobles hunted water birds on the banks of the Nile, or rode on chariots into the desert to hunt for lions, ostriches and cobras. Sometimes hunters formed a team to spear a hippo and catch it in a net. Other noblemen preferred to stay at home, and fish in their own garden pools.

▶ In this painting of a banquet, servant girls dance for the guests and serve them food. Servants also placed cones of perfumed fat on the guests' heads. The cones gradually melted, creating a sweet smell.

SPORT AND GAMES

The Egyptians loved to compete against each other in athletic contests. Ancient Egyptian sports included boxing, gymnastics, running, rowing, jumping, and throwing the javelin. People played a kind of hockey, using palm tree branches for sticks and a leather ball stuffed with papyrus. They also formed teams for energetic tugs-of-war, in which each team pulled as hard as they could to show they were the strongest.

When they were not playing sports, Egyptians of all ages liked to relax at home with a board game. One of the most popular games was 'senet'. It had a set of pieces that were moved across a board, rather like the modern game of backgammon.

REAL LIVES

NEBAMUN: A NOBLE WHO LOVED TO HUNT

Nebamun was a nobleman who died around 1400 BC. In a painting in his tomb (shown here) he is seen hunting for birds in the marshes of the River Nile. Nebamun is shown holding a throwing stick, which was used to stun the birds. Also in the painting are his wife and daughter and his handsome ginger cat. Nebamun's cat would have been specially trained to frighten the birds from their hiding place.

HOW IMPORTANT WAS RELIGION FOR THE EGYPTIANS?

The Ancient Egyptians worshipped dozens of gods and goddesses. Every village had its own shrine, where people could say prayers and leave offerings to the gods. There were also massive temples on the banks of the Nile. On feast days, priests carried statues of the gods around towns and cities, while people sang songs and prayed. Then the priests **sacrificed** animals to the gods.

▲ This carving shows a man presenting an offering to a sacred bull. Behind the bull stands the goddess Isis.

TALKING TO THE GODS

Everybody in Ancient Egypt tried to follow the will of the gods. If they had to make a big decision in their lives, they paid a scribe to write down their question for the god. This request was handed to a priest who disappeared into the temple and returned with an answer. Then the grateful people left a gift of thanks to the gods.

PREPARING FOR THE NEXT WORLD

The Egyptians believed that, after they died, they would go to the next world to live with the gods. This belief led them to bury the dead with great care (see page 21). Embalmers preserved the bodies of people of all classes and even favourite pets. People were often buried with their possessions, so that they would have everything they needed in the next world.

SERVANTS OF THE GODS

Some men and women devoted their lives to the gods. Women often worked as musicians and dancers in the temples. Male priests conducted ceremonies and wrote sacred texts. Some priests and priestesses worked in large temples, which contained a statue of a god or goddess. Every morning, they 'woke' the statue. Then they washed and dressed it, offered it food and prayed to it.

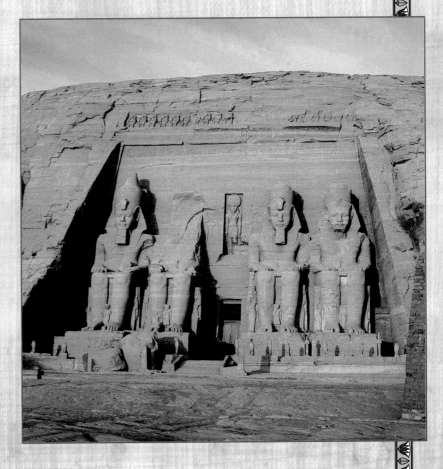

▶ Pharaoh Ramses II built two magnificent temples at Abu Simbel in honour of the gods. These four giant figures carved from the rock represent Ramses and three other gods.

REAL LIVES

THUYA: A PRIESTESS

Thuya was the **high priestess** of the rain god Min. She was married to Yuya, the high priest of Min. The couple were important people at the court of Pharaoh Amenhotep III. (Yuya was in charge of the royal chariots.) Later, their daughter Tiy became Queen of Egypt. Thuya's golden mummy case shows a round-faced woman with a very contented smile.

Glossary

archaeologist Someone who learns about the past by examining old buildings and objects.

chancellor The person in charge of a country's money.

civilization A well-organized society.

dynasty A ruling family.

embalmer Someone who prepares the bodies of the dead for burial.

fertile Good for growing crops.

general A leader of soldiers in an army.

hieroglyph A picture or a symbol that represents an object, a letter, or a sound.

high priest/ priestess A very important man/woman priest.

inscription A carved message, often on a tomb.

internal organs Body parts, such as the heart or the stomach, that are on the inside of the body.

irrigate To supply water to crops.

mineral A substance, such as iron and salt, which is found under the earth.

minister Someone in charge of a government department.

mummy A body that has been specially treated and then wrapped in bandages, to stop it from decaying.

next world A place where the dead go after their life on earth, according to Ancient Egyptian beliefs.

official Someone who holds an important position in a government.

papyrus A kind of paper made from a reed-like plant.

pharaoh An Egyptian king.

regent Someone who rules on behalf of the real ruler of a country.

sacrifice To kill an animal and offer it as a gift to a god.

scribe Someone who copies out letters and other documents by hand.

viceroy Someone who acts as a deputy to a ruler, taking charge of part of their land. A viceroy governed Nubia, a territory to the south of Ancient Egypt.

vizier Someone who acts as a deputy to a ruler, taking charge of part of their land. Two viziers governed Upper and Lower Egypt.

FURTHER INFORMATION

MORE BOOKS TO READ

Jane Shuter
History Starts Here:
The Ancient Egyptians
(Wayland, 2008)

Clive Gifford
Food and Cooking In:
Ancient Egypt
(Wayland, 2009)

Stewart Ross
Find Out About:
Ancient Egypt
(Wayland, 2006)

Jane Shuter
History Beneath Your Feet:
Ancient Egypt
(Wayland, 2008)

John Malam
Ancient Egyptian Jobs
(Heinemann Library, 2002)

USEFUL WEBSITES

http://www.ancientegypt.co.uk/menu.html
A very well illustrated site from the British Museum, including sections on pharaohs and trades.

http://www.iwebquest.com/egypt/ancientegypt.htm
A well-organized site for children, with lots of projects.

http://www.mnsu.edu/emuseum/prehistory/egypt/
A large site including sections on daily life, religion, history and art.

http://www.egyptologyonline.com/introduction.htm
A well-illustrated site, with sections on many different aspects of life in Ancient Egypt.

PLACES TO VISIT

The British Museum, London, UK
A very large collection of mummies, coffins and carvings

The Pitt-Rivers Museum, Oxford, UK
Several interesting mummies, including some mummified cats

The Egyptian Museum, Cairo, Egypt
The best collection in the world of treasures excavated from Ancient Egyptian tombs, including the golden mummies of Tutankhamun

The Metropolitan Museum
New York, USA
A large collection of Ancient Egyptian objects, including carvings, jewellery and tomb models

INDEX

Numbers in **bold** indicate pictures.